Venus

Earth

Asteroid Belt

Saturn

Neptune

Project
Gemini

Project

Gemini

Ray Spangenburg and Kit Moser

Franklin Watts

A DIVISION OF GROLIER PUBLISHING
NEW YORK · LONDON · HONG KONG · SYDNEY
DANBURY, CONNECTICUT

In memory of
LLOYD SPANGENBURG,
who helped make dreams fly

Photographs ©: AP/Wide World Photos: 60; NASA: cover, 2, 8, 13, 15, 16, 18, 20, 22, 24, 27, 28, 30, 34, 35, 37, 39, 47, 48, 53, 55, 58, 59, 62, 64, 69, 74, 75, 82, 83, 85, 89, 96, 101, 102, 105; Sovfoto/Eastfoto: 43 (Itar-Tass), 10, 12, 14, 31, 67, 94.
Map by: Bob Italiano

The photograph on the cover shows astronaut Edward H. White performing a space walk or EVA (extravehicular activity) during the *Gemini 5* flight. The photo opposite the title page shows Ed White in the Gemini capsule.

Visit Franklin Watts on the Internet at:
http://publishing.grolier.com

Library of Congress Cataloging-in-Publication Data

Spangenburg, Ray.
    Project Gemini / by Ray Spangenburg and Kit Moser.
        p. cm.—(Out of this world)
    Includes bibliographical references and index.
    Summary: Discusses the importance of the twelve Gemini space flights that laid the foundation for the United States exploration of space.
    ISBN 0-531-11762-6 (lib. bdg.)   0-531-13973-5 (pbk.)
    1. Project Gemini (U.S.) —History—Juvenile literature. [1. Project Gemini (U.S.) 2. Space flights.] I. Moser, Diane, 1944- II. Title. III. Out of this world (Franklin Watts, inc.)

TL789.8.U6G775   2001
629.45'4'0973—dc21   00-027007

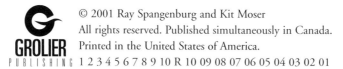

Acknowledgments

We would like to thank the many people who have contributed to *Project Gemini*. First of all, special appreciation goes to Melissa Stewart, our editor at Franklin Watts, whose steady flow of creativity, energy, enthusiasm, and dedication have infused this series. We would also like to thank NASA Chief Historian Roger D. Launius and Sam Storch, Lecturer at the American Museum-Hayden Planetarium, who both looked over the manuscript and made many much-appreciated suggestions. Also, to Tony Reichhardt and John Rhea, once our editors at the former *Space World Magazine,* thanks for starting us out on the fascinating journey we have taken during our years of writing about space.

Contents

A Gemini spacecraft lifts off from Launch Pad 19 at Kennedy Space Center in Cape Canaveral, Florida.

Chapter 1

Gemini: Spacecraft Built for Two

Most people know about Project Mercury (1961–1963)—the pioneering spaceflights that put the first U.S. astronauts in space. Project Apollo (1968–1972)—the program that put the first humans on the Moon—is even more famous. Yet many people have never heard of Project Gemini, the twelve important and exciting missions between these two "firsts."

Project Gemini was exciting, intense, and challenging. Without it, no Apollo missions would have flown, and no one would have gone to the Moon. Between March 1965 and November 1966, ten pairs of Gemini astronauts flew into space. These astronauts were among the most skillful in space history. They performed courageous feats and daring firsts. They paved the way for everything accomplished by Apollo and all the Moon missions that followed. This book tells the Gemini story—a vital and exciting step in America's journey to the Moon.

The Great Space Race

For centuries, people had dreamed of voyages to the Moon and traveling in space. By the middle of the twentieth century, technological advances made this vision a reality. On October 4, 1957, the former Soviet Union, also known as the Union of Soviet Socialist Republics (USSR), sent the first *satellite* into space. The launch of *Sputnik 1* thrust the world into a new era—the space age.

The Sputnik launch both amazed and frightened the rest of the world. The feat required tremendous rocket power and technological ability. Scientists and government officials in the United States had known the Soviet Union was working on a satellite—the United States was too. However, most people assumed the United States would beat the Soviets to space. The *Sputnik 1* launch was a big blow to American prestige.

The Soviet Union launched *Sputnik 1* on October 4, 1957.

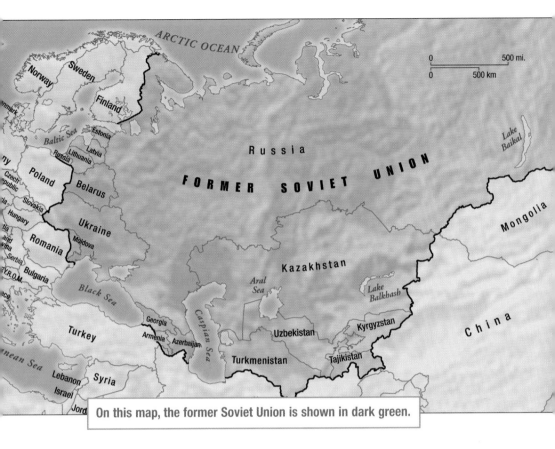

On this map, the former Soviet Union is shown in dark green.

In addition, it seemed to show that the Soviet Union was more powerful and better organized than any other nation in the world, and that could mean big trouble. If the Soviets had the rocket power to launch a satellite into *orbit*, they also must have the power to send nuclear warheads anywhere in the world.

The Soviet Union had formed following the Russian Revolution of 1917 by uniting Russia, Ukraine, Belarus, and several other countries in Central Asia, Eastern Europe, and the Balkan Peninsula. The Russian Communist Party quickly gained power over the central government, and that nation later developed into a tyrannical dictatorship.

Following World War II (1939–1945), the Soviet Union became one of the strongest forces in the world.

Until the Soviet Union dissolved in 1991, most non-Communist countries viewed Soviet power as an enormous threat to freedom and democracy. As a result, a "Cold War" developed between the Soviet Union and the United States. The Cold War consisted of many hostile and threatening gestures, but few "hot," fighting battles. Instead, it was primarily a fight for prestige in the eyes of the world. The launch of *Sputnik 1* was therefore technologically exciting, but politically chilling. A "space race" began, and the United States quickly responded to the challenge.

Birth of a Space Program

The United States had also been working toward launching a satellite, so jumping the hurdle to space would take only a few months. However, before the United States could show its stuff, the Soviet Union launched a second, even larger satellite. *Sputnik 2* zoomed into space in November 1957. The American people did not like being behind. They became more determined than ever to launch a satellite of their own.

The Soviet Union launched *Sputnik 2* just 1 month after *Sputnik 1*.

After a failed attempt in December, the United States finally sent its first satellite into space on January 31, 1958. *Explorer 1* soared into space propelled by a Juno 1 rocket. The United States had entered the space race.

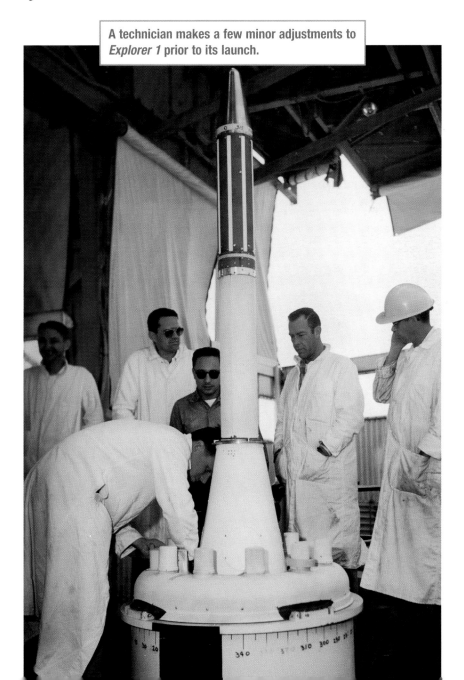

A technician makes a few minor adjustments to *Explorer 1* prior to its launch.

By October 1958, a new federal agency opened its doors in Washington, D.C. Its unwieldy official name, the National Aeronautics and Space Administration, soon became shortened to just NASA. Its purpose was to run the U.S. space program. The job would prove both challenging and exciting. By December, NASA announced its first big project. It would send a human being into space. This ambitious undertaking would be called Project Mercury, and it would become the new agency's primary focus for the next few years.

Meanwhile, the Soviet Union had not been idle, and before the United States could put its first astronaut in space, the Soviets launched cosmonaut Yuri Gagarin into Earth orbit. On April 12, 1961, Gagarin's Vostok spacecraft circled the planet once and landed safely near the Volga River. Again, the world was amazed and fascinated.

Yuri Gagarin aboard *Vostok 1*

Project Mercury would be ready to launch its first astronaut on May 5. That was just a few weeks later—but once again the United States had missed out on first place. The Mercury launch was also not as ambitious as Gagarin's flight. Gagarin made a complete orbit around the planet and spent 108 minutes in space. The first Mercury flight did not reach Earth orbit and lasted only 15 minutes.

Still, when the first Mercury spacecraft lifted off, the moment tasted sweet. Astronaut Alan Shepard's *Freedom 7* rode to space on an Atlas rocket and returned safely to Earth in an exciting splashdown in the

Astronaut Alan Shepard waits for his Mercury spacecraft to launch.

Atlantic Ocean. He and his spacecraft were plucked from the water by a helicopter and carried to a waiting aircraft carrier. Two days later, President John F. Kennedy awarded Shepard NASA's Distinguished Service Medal. The United States and NASA had accomplished their first goal.

Shortly after Alan Shepard's historic space flight, the NASA Administrator and the secretary of defense wrote a long memo to President John F. Kennedy. It was classified at the time because of national security concerns, but historians now know that it concluded: "Our attainments are a major element in the international competition between the Soviet system and our own. . . . Projects such as lunar and planetary exploration are, in this sense, part of the battle along the fluid front of the Cold War." Moreover, they pointed out, "It is man, not merely machines, in space that captures the imagination of the world."

President John F. Kennedy (right) awarding Alan Shepard (left) NASA's Distinguished Service Medal

Communications and weather satellites would certainly prove useful. However, a truly ambitious project involving humans in space would make a much more powerful statement to the world. It would show off U.S. technological power. It would also display the nation's ability to muster resources and manage an incredibly complex and challenging undertaking. The two men recommended the ultimate grandstand play in the giant public relations contest with the Soviet Union—landing astronauts on the Moon. Kennedy liked the idea.

On May 25, 1961, President Kennedy announced to a joint session of Congress and the American people: "I believe that this nation should commit itself to achieving the goal, before this decade is out, of landing a man on the Moon and returning him safely to Earth."

With these words, Kennedy significantly stepped up the space race between the United States and the Soviet Union. In the coming years, each side would try to "one-up" the other in successive displays of high-tech, challenging space feats. However, Kennedy had set the ultimate goal line: Humans would leave Earth, land on the Moon, and return safely.

The United States saw the international stakes clearly: To achieve this goal first would go far toward winning the battle "between freedom and tyranny," as Kennedy put it to Congress that day. NASA and the nation geared up. Kennedy intended to give the American people, literally, the Moon.

Plans for the Moon

At NASA, new plans began to take shape immediately. America's journey to the Moon would have three big steps—Project Mercury, Project Gemini, and Project Apollo.

On February 20, 1962, John Glenn and his *Friendship 7* Mercury capsule zoomed into space.

An Atlas rocket thrusts *Friendship 7* into space.

The first step was to build a spacecraft and rocket to carry a human being into space and safely back to Earth. The first Project Mercury flight had already accomplished this goal. Five more Mercury missions would expand on Shepard's flight, including John Glenn's flight in orbit—judged by many people as the first real U.S. spaceflight.

Ultimately, NASA had to set the stage for missions to the Moon—Project Apollo. The Moon missions would take detailed planning. They would require a far bigger rocket than any the United States, or the Soviet Union, had built so far. They would also require a much more complex spacecraft. Rocket engineers, led by Wernher von Braun, rolled up their sleeves, and spacecraft designers sharpened their pencils. There was plenty of work to do.

In the meantime, astronauts had to learn how to control spacecraft in the weightlessness of space. They also needed to prove they could venture into the harsh environment on space walks and perform repairs in weightlessness. For the Moon missions, astronauts would need to know how to fly up to another spacecraft without colliding, *dock* with it, and undock. That's where Project Gemini came in. It would give astronauts an opportunity to try out every major maneuver and task required for the Apollo missions.

A True Spacecraft

The Gemini capsule was bigger than the tiny Mercury spacecraft. Like the Mercury capsule, the Gemini spacecraft was shaped like a bell. This spacecraft, though, had room for two and was a handsome white with black trim.* It could transport pairs of astronauts into space and

* The name Gemini means "twins" in Latin.

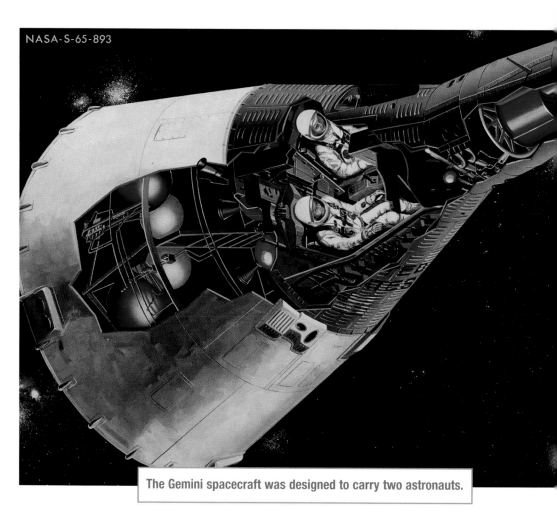

The Gemini spacecraft was designed to carry two astronauts.

sustain them for up to 14 days (the time it would take to go to the Moon and back).

The Gemini capsule was about 19 feet (5.8 m) long—not much larger than most living rooms and smaller than many. It had a narrow, cylindrical nose at the front and flared out to a flat bottom about 10 feet (3 m) wide at the base.

The docking mechanism and parachutes for reentry were located in the nose of the capsule. Behind that was the crew's cabin, the heart of the capsule. The cabin had about 50 percent more room than the

Fuel Cells: Energy Source of the Future?

Project Gemini's engineers were the first to make serious use of the fuel cell, an unusual energy source that had been around since 1839. In that year, a Welsh judge named Sir William Grove built the first fuel cell, which is basically a lot like a battery. It uses simple chemicals—just hydrogen and oxygen—to produce electricity.

A fuel cell is made up of two *electrodes* sandwiched around an *electrolyte*. The fuel can be a hydrocarbon fuel, which is then processed to produce hydrogen, or it can be hydrogen itself. The hydrogen (H_2) reacts with oxygen (O_2) in the fuel cell and generates electric power. The by-product of the process is water (H_2O).

NASA contractors refined the concept, and the fuel cell became one of Project Gemini's great success stories. Fuel cells were also used by the Apollo spacecraft and are still used today to provide electricity and water aboard the Space Shuttle.

Some environmentalists think fuel cells could replace gasoline combustion engines in automobiles—solving many of the problems caused by engines that run on fossil fuels and fill the air with carbon dioxide. Even water-vapor output is lower from fuel cells than from gasoline combustion, and a fuel cell running on renewable hydrogen produces no carbon dioxide at all. The fuel cell could end up being one of Gemini's most important legacies.

Mercury capsule, but still it wasn't much larger than a phone booth— or the front seat of a Volkswagen, as astronaut Frank Borman put it. It was almost completely filled by the two astronaut couches placed side by side.

During reentry, both sections of the base were jettisoned, or discarded, when they were no longer needed. Then the series of parachutes in the nose opened, and the spacecraft slowed. The pilot could position the landing somewhat by rolling the spacecraft and adding *lift*.

The base of the capsule had two compartments. The retrograde section contained four retrorockets that fired in reverse to provide brakes as the spacecraft reentered Earth's atmosphere at the end of its

A spacecraft can't be launched into orbit by just any rocket. The rocket has to be powerful enough to lift the spacecraft away from Earth's gravity and achieve a speed of 4.5 miles (7.2 km) per second. That's faster than a speeding bullet!

Reaching that speed isn't easy, and a single engine isn't powerful enough to lift itself plus a spacecraft into orbit. So, from the Soviet *Sputnik 1* satellite on, engineers have used multistage rockets. In fact, long before the first Sputnik was launched, early rocket pioneers had recognized the need for the boost that multistage rockets can provide.

Early in the twentieth century, Russian theorist Konstantin Tsiolkovsky wrote about using multistage rockets to achieve orbit. In the United States, rocket pioneer Robert Goddard launched his first multistage rocket by 1914.

A multistage rocket has two or more rocket engines, often a smaller one stacked on top of a larger one. The first rocket fires and then drops away after its fuel is used up, leaving much less weight for the next rocket stage to lift. Then that engine ignites, burns, and drops away. The maximum speed achieved is the sum of the final speeds achieved by all the rockets—a much greater speed than would be possible with a single rocket, even a huge one.

U.S. rocket pioneer Robert Goddard poses with a rocket he completed in 1925.

mission. Below the retrograde section was the adapter section. It stored the fuel cells for the spacecraft's electric power supply and reserve oxygen for the crew. The adapter also had another very important piece of equipment—the Orbital Attitude and Maneuvering System (OAMS), sixteen engines that could be used to maneuver the capsule. The OAMS made Gemini a much better spacecraft than Mercury.

Some people jokingly referred to the Mercury astronauts as "Spam in a can." In other words, they were like helpless chopped meat traveling in a craft no more manageable than an inert can. Gemini was different.

It gave the astronauts, all former jet pilots, a real chance to use their flight experience and skills. Years later, astronaut Buzz Aldrin called Gemini "a true spacecraft meant to voyage in space."

Titan Power

The Gemini spacecraft was more than twice as heavy as the Mercury spacecraft. The Atlas rocket used to launch the one-person Mercury missions could not lift such a heavy load. So NASA turned to the Titan II, an Air Force *intercontinental ballistic missile (ICBM)*. This is one example of the help the U.S. space program often obtained from the military, and vice versa, in a long, cooperative relationship.

The big Titan II stood about 103 feet (31.4 m) tall and had a diameter of 10 feet (3 m). It could lift about 8,000 pounds (3,630 kg). This capacity set the limit for the total weight of the fully loaded Gemini—including astronauts. Like the Atlas, the Titan II was a *multistage rocket*. The first stage consisted of two engines that each gave a thrust of 216,000 pounds (98,000 kg). The second stage picked up where the first left off and provided a thrust of 100,300 pounds (45,500 kg).

The mighty Titan II propels a Gemini spacecraft into orbit.

The Titan II was the largest U.S. launch vehicle available at the time. Wernher von Braun and his team were working on a huge rocket, called Saturn V, but it was still a couple of years away from being ready. NASA planned to use its power for the demanding Apollo missions to the Moon.

Chapter 2

Getting Ready

As the Mercury program continued its missions, the Gemini space-craft began to take shape. Its design was heavily influenced by Gus Grissom. Grissom cared passionately about every detail, especially the spacecraft's controls.

Gus Grissom had been the pilot of the second Mercury capsule, *Liberty Bell 7*. With his mission completed early in the program, he considered what he should concentrate on next. He knew NASA planned to give each of the seven astronauts a flight before anyone flew a second mission. So he recognized that he would not have another chance to go to space until the Gemini program began. With that, as Wally Schirra later recalled, Grissom announced, "I'm going to go up to St. Louis and play with Gemini."

Astronaut Gus Grissom prepares to enter his Mercury spacecraft, *Liberty Bell 7*.

The Gemini spacecraft was being designed and built at the McDonnell Aircraft Corporation plant in St. Louis, Missouri. Instead of training for a second Mercury mission he would never fly, Grissom was on hand at the plant to oversee the design and construction of Gemini. That's why the astronauts called the new capsule the "Gus-mobile." Grissom's idea of "playing" was most people's idea of work. He intended to help make Gemini a space flier's dream.

Gus Grissom and John Young wait patiently while technicians make adjustments to the *Gemini* capsule.

"Gus really had a big hand in everything, from the way the cock-pit was laid out to what instruments went where," Gemini astronaut John Young would recall later. "It was his baby." He and Grissom tried out this baby on its first flight, the Gemini 3 mission, with Grissom as command pilot and Young as pilot.

Grissom wanted to make sure that Mercury's drawbacks didn't show up again in Gemini, and he hovered over the project. "All I had to do was say 'No, I don't like it' or 'Yeah, it's okay,'" Grissom said in *Life* magazine. Having an astronaut so closely involved in the design process paid off both for NASA and for the other astronauts—most of the time. Unfortunately for some, the design followed not only Grissom's pointers, but also his physical form.

Grissom spent long hours sitting in the mock-up to make sure the astronauts' physical surroundings would work well during flight. In the process, however, the designers ended up practically forming the capsule's interior to fit Grissom's 5-foot, 7-inch (170-centimeter) body. When the other astronauts tried it out, fourteen out of sixteen of them didn't fit, and room had to be carved out for those with longer legs and taller frames.

The Gusmobile had to be compact and trim enough to stay within the Titan rocket's maximum-weight limit. The fuel alone weighed 1,000 pounds (454 kg)—more fuel than either Mercury or the Soviet Union's Vostok spacecraft ever carried. The total weight of everything else had to come in at 7,000 pounds (3,175 kg)—including the heat shield, parachutes, retrorockets and attitude jets, computer, guidance and control systems, life-support system including oxygen, all other equipment, and, of course, the astronauts.

The astronauts liked flying the Gusmobile. It was a pilot's dream. Pete Conrad was a former Navy test pilot who flew two Gemini flights, and in his opinion the Gemini spacecraft reminded him of a high-performance fighter. "You did everything manually," he remarked years later. "You flew it."

Three for the Price of One

On April 8, 1964, *Gemini 1* lifted off with no passengers onboard. This crewless test flight orbited Earth for 4 days and splashed down successfully. The Gemini spacecraft's orbit and reentry systems worked perfectly.

As NASA prepared to send piloted Gemini missions into space, the Soviets looked for a way to outdo the United States. They were in

On April 8, 1964, the *Gemini 1* test flight zoomed into space and orbited Earth four times.

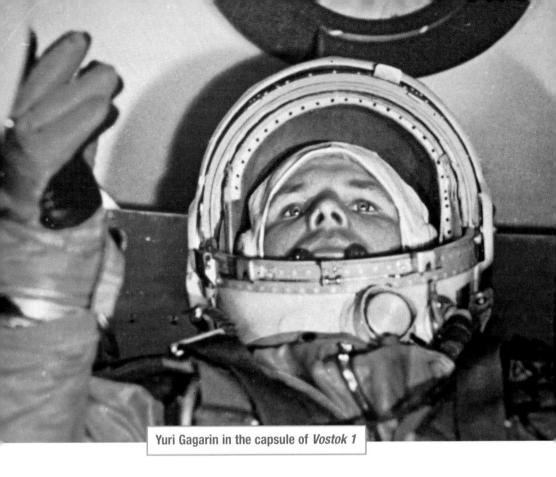

Yuri Gagarin in the capsule of _Vostok 1_

the middle of building a new spacecraft that would carry three cosmonauts at a time. The spacecraft was not even close to being ready yet, but Soviet Premier Nikita Khrushchev called for a demonstration that would put three cosmonauts in space by November 7, 1964.

No Soviet official could afford to ignore such an order. So the Soviet space program's chief designer, Sergei Korolev, had only one choice. He had to find a way to send three cosmonauts into space in one spacecraft. All he had available was a Vostok capsule like the one that sent Gagarin and other cosmonauts into space one at a time. It was the Soviet equal of the Mercury spacecraft—small and simple. Three people would be a very tight squeeze. Everything they could possibly do without was left behind.

Korolev had to make a lot of design compromises, and he didn't like that—he was an excellent designer, the heart of the Soviet space program, and a man of high standards. In addition, the three men had to fly in regular clothes, without the protection of baggy spacesuits. The cosmonauts had food for only 24 hours, instead of the usual 10-day supply. Korolev also had to remove the ejector seat. If anything went wrong early in the flight, the crew had no escape route. The plan skimped dangerously on safety, but it could do the job.

On October 12, 1964, three cosmonauts rode into space squeezed together in this little spacecraft. It now had a new name—*Voskhod 1*. They landed safely about 24 hours later, and they made history. The crew included the first physician in space, a prominent Soviet scientist, and a commander who was a trained cosmonaut. The choice of prominent crew members suggested to the rest of the world that the Soviets were confident about the spacecraft's safety. The media worldwide applauded enthusiastically.

Some close watchers of the Soviet space program could see that the *Voskhod 1* flight was a sleight of hand. However, the truth about this and many other aspects of the Soviet space program were not widely known until after the Soviet Union dissolved in 1991. At the time, the Soviet Union seemed to have raced ahead of the United States once again.

A few months later, on January 19, 1965, *Gemini 2* lifted off for an 18-minute suborbital test of the heat shield. It worked perfectly. NASA officials were convinced that Gemini was ready for its first astronauts.

Chapter 3

Flying Gemini

When astronauts Gus Grissom and John Young arrived at Cape Canaveral on the morning of March 23, 1965, everything except the weather looked ready to go. Their day had started before 5:00 A.M. They had already downed the now traditional steak-and-eggs astronauts' launch-day breakfast and suited up. Once inside the first piloted Gusmobile, the two astronauts waited.

What's in a Name?

The official name of Grissom and Young's spacecraft was Gemini 3, also known as GT3 (for *Gemini-Titan 3*, combining the names of the spacecraft and its launch rocket). Grissom, however, had given it another name. He called it *Molly Brown*—and the name stuck. NASA

John Young (left) and Gus Grissom (right) pose for a publicity shot.

wasn't crazy about the name, maybe because it didn't sound dignified, or maybe because it alluded to a fiasco NASA didn't want the public or Congress to recall—the sinking of Grissom's Mercury capsule, *Liberty Bell 7*.

Grissom wanted to pay tribute to *Liberty Bell 7*, and at the same time assert that his Gemini capsule would not sink. So he named the capsule after Molly Brown, a character in a popular Broadway play, *The Unsinkable Molly Brown*. The play was later made into a movie starring Debbie Reynolds, who played the title character, a woman who survived the tragic sinking of the great oceangoing vessel, the *Titanic*. In fact, since NASA didn't like *Molly Brown*, Grissom suggested naming the capsule *Titanic* instead.

NASA decided *Molly Brown* would do. The astronauts did not name the rest of the Gemini missions, however. *Molly Brown* had raised too many complaints from members of Congress who were worried about image. From then on, the program's spacecraft went strictly by "Gemini" plus a Roman numeral. However, most newspaper reporters used Arabic numerals, referring to the spacecraft as *Gemini 4*, *Gemini 5*, and so on for ease and consistency.

On Their Way

Molly Brown's liftoff was smooth and quiet. Grissom and Young were surprised to see the mission clock running—timing the length of the mission, which had already started—and to hear fellow astronaut Gordon Cooper announce liftoff from Mission Control. They felt pressure equal to six times Earth's normal gravity for $2\frac{1}{2}$ minutes. Then the first-stage rocket engine finished its job and cut off.

The Gemini capsule nicknamed *Molly Brown* was thrust into space by a Titan rocket on March 23, 1965. Gus Grissom and John Young went along for the ride.

Suddenly, as the second-stage engine lit, Young saw the spacecraft bathed in orange-yellow light, and he felt a twinge of concern. Not only was this the first time out for the Gusmobile with a crew aboard, it was also Young's first spaceflight. But he quickly realized the source of the light was normal.

After calming down a bit, Young looked around. The view of Earth's horizon out the spacecraft window was entrancing, and the rapid motion and power from the thrust of the second-stage engine was more exhilarating than any theme-park ride.

The second-stage engine shut down $5\frac{1}{2}$ minutes after launch, and Young heard what sounded like heavy cannon fire. It was the sound of the small, controlled blasts that popped the second-stage rocket loose from Gemini. Now, the astronauts took control. Grissom fired the rear *thrusters* to nudge the spacecraft into its planned orbit. This kind of control was not possible aboard Mercury—so the astronauts were already putting Gemini's new maneuverability to work.

The moment was exciting. It was the first solid proof that astronauts could fly a spacecraft well enough to do the fancy maneuvers necessary for a Moon mission.

Changing Orbit

Then Grissom turned *Molly Brown* around to face in the opposite direction in the line of flight. He fired the thrusters again with careful precision, just enough to slow the spacecraft a little. This maneuver put Gemini into a nearly round orbit around Earth. This proved that an astronaut could change a spacecraft's orbit, so that it would be pos-

Gus Grissom: First-Class Flight Tester

Gus Grissom was one of NASA's most trusted astronauts—despite the sinking of *Liberty Bell 7* during the Mercury program. Grissom's role in the Gemini program's space-capsule design was central to its success. Later, he was chosen commander of *Apollo 1* to test that equipment out. Like Wally Schirra, Grissom spanned all three programs. Unfortunately, Grissom never got to fly the Apollo spacecraft. He died with fellow crew members Ed White and Roger Chaffee in a tragic launchpad fire during a test of the *Apollo 1* command module on January 27, 1967.

Gus Grissom (center) was chosen to be the commander of *Apollo 1*. But the flight never made it to space. He and fellow crew members Ed White (left) and Roger Chaffee (right) died in an accident during a preflight test.

sible for two spacecraft to *rendezvous*—meet in space—even if they did not start out in the same orbit.

The astronauts were all crack test pilots who loved using their flying skills. So for them, and for the Apollo program, improved maneuverability was the most important difference between the Mercury and Gemini spacecraft. Using the 25-pound (11.3-kg) thrusters at the rear of the adapter section, they could truly control the spacecraft and even change its orbit, as Grissom had just done.

On Mercury, the astronauts could make a few adjustments with the controls. On Gemini they could not only turn and change the capsule's *attitude* and *pitch*, but they could also control the path of the spacecraft. For the four Mercury astronauts who entered orbit, the rocket launch determined what orbit they entered, Earth's gravity held them there during flight, and the retrorockets determined their path for coming back down. Most of this was directed by automatic computer control. Now, automatic control was still available as a choice, but Gemini could be flown manually—"by a stick"—and that made these former jet test pilots very happy.

Gauging Trouble

Everything looked good, really good—at least for the first 20 minutes of *Molly Brown*'s flight. Then, just as the spacecraft passed out of reach of the mid-Atlantic tracking stations and could no longer get advice from the ground, Young noticed the oxygen pressure gauge showed a sudden drop. His first thought was that the system supplying the oxygen was in trouble. Then he glanced at several other gauges and noticed problems with them too. He realized the trouble might not be with any of the systems being monitored—a

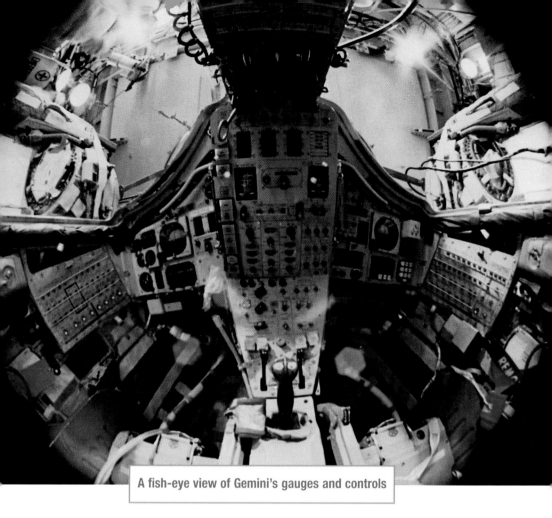

A fish-eye view of Gemini's gauges and controls

defective power supply was a more likely culprit. He deftly switched to a secondary power supply and the problem disappeared. Thanks to preflight training and calm, quick thinking, Young solved the problem in just 45 seconds.

Corned Beef, Anyone?

It was a short flight—a test run to try out the new equipment. The astronauts did a couple of bioscience experiments (one of which Grissom broke) and tested some freeze-dried space food as part of their assignment, but no real meal was planned.

At one point, Young calmly asked Grissom if he'd like some corned beef. "Sure, sounds good," Grissom replied. So Young handed him a tightly compacted corned beef sandwich made the night before at a delicatessen near the launch site in Florida. Young had smuggled it aboard. Grissom was amused, took a couple of bites, and then wrapped it back up. Then he noticed that a couple of crumbs of bread had broken off the sandwich.

Crumbs in space are worse than crumbs in bed—instead of falling to the floor, they float weightlessly around and get into everything from an astronaut's nose to a spacecraft's precision controls. Luckily, in this case, no harm was done.

This story has become one of the best-known sagas of the early astronaut days. Wally Schirra later confessed to supplying the sandwich as a joke. NASA and the government watchdogs were not amused. What went on the spacecraft and what the astronauts ate onboard was supposed to be tightly controlled. This was a billion-dollar program, and astronaut antics did not amuse those who were watching the bills.

As punishment, Young received neither a medal nor the customary promotion after the mission—those honors would have to wait until after his next mission. He was a top-flight astronaut, however, and NASA authorities knew that. In June 1966, after his second Gemini flight, he received the recognition he deserved. He was also given several more key assignments later on.

Back to Earth

Astronauts onboard Mercury spacecraft had no control over their flight path and no control over reentry. Gemini pilots could alter their angle during reentry and splashdown. To do this, they had a capability called "lift," which enabled them to extend their flight path by as much as 300 miles (480 km). They could also alter the course to the right or to the left by as much as 50 miles (80 km).

This control would be critical during the Apollo missions. When Apollo spacecraft returned from the Moon, they would be traveling at enormous speeds, and their unadjusted angle would be steep.

Grissom and Young splashed down smoothly—at least until the parachute took on water and dragged the spacecraft under. For a moment, Grissom had the feeling that he might really go down this time, a frightening reminder of his less than perfect *Liberty Bell 7* splashdown. But once the parachute was released, *Gemini 3* righted itself and bobbed back to the surface. They were safe, although Young—who had been a Navy pilot—was quick to observe that Gemini was no boat. Once afloat, the capsule heaved and pitched wildly. Both astronauts got seasick. To Grissom, though, Gemini had driven like a Corvette—and he was happy.

Chapter 4

Space Walk and a Covered Wagon

Of the world's all-time greatest human adventures, the first space walk—floating in the vast openness of space surrounded by infinite blackness—would have to be high on anyone's list. Learning to work outside a spacecraft, protected only by a spacesuit, was one of Project Gemini's primary goals, and Edward White was the astronaut chosen to try it out.

However, White would not be the first person in history to perform a space walk—that honor went to Alexei Leonov of the Soviet Union. Once again, the Soviet Union trumped the United States. The acrobatic cosmonaut had ventured outside his spacecraft on March 18, 1965, a few days before Grissom and Young's first Gem-

This photo of cosmonaut Alexei Leonov was taken at the Yuri Gagarin statue in 1999.

ini flight. Leonov's brave encounter with the hazards of space was another point in the Soviet Union's tally of firsts, and a major disappointment for NASA.

Leonov's venture did not make White's job any easier or less dangerous though. The Soviets kept nearly every detail of their space experiences secret. They did not share their knowledge with the rest of the world—and especially not with their primary Cold War adversary, the United States. So, for NASA's astronauts, even "second-place" achievements always held enormous uncertainty. The first U.S. *extravehicular activity (EVA)* was no exception.

Stepping Out in Space

As the *Gemini 4* launch date drew near, NASA officials became increasingly concerned. Ed White's special pressurized suit and other equipment for a full EVA were still not ready. For awhile, NASA officials weren't sure if the space walk would take place. Finally, though, just 6 days before the planned launch date, all the pieces were in place. Ed White's space walk was a certainty.

White had never doubted that the equipment would be ready. He had been preparing for this part of the mission for months. He had worked in a high-altitude pressure chamber in St. Louis—the closest anybody on Earth could come to simulating the vacuum of space. By the time of liftoff, he was in excellent physical condition and ready to "walk."

Liftoff took place on June 3, with Jim McDivitt as commander. This was the first mission directed from NASA's new Manned Spacecraft Center in Houston, Texas. It was also the first liftoff ever televised internationally—broadcast to twelve European nations via *Early Bird*, a communications satellite.

Gemini 4's flight plan called for McDivitt to turn the capsule around during the first orbit and dock with the emptied second stage of the Titan II rocket that had launched the spacecraft. However, that part of the mission did not go well. Every time McDivitt turned his thrusters on to chase after the rocket, his target seemed to bounce away. What McDivitt didn't realize was that using his thrusters placed him in a higher orbit. As a result, the more he chased his target, the farther it seemed to retreat.*

Originally, White planned to complete his EVA after the capsule had docked with the empty launch vehicle. He would exit *Gemini 4* and go visit the Titan II rocket. But because *Gemini 4* had used up half its fuel trying to play catch-up in orbit, White and McDivitt had to abandon this part of the mission.

Instead, the astronauts went on to Ed White's space walk, which went beautifully. On the third orbit, the astronauts partially depressurized the cabin and tested their spacesuit pressure. On Earth, we live at the bottom of a deep layer of atmosphere, and our bodies need the presence of air and air pressure. In the vacuum of space, however, there is no atmosphere and no atmospheric pressure. We couldn't live, even for a moment, without a pressurized suit or spacecraft to protect our organs from bursting. That's one reason an EVA is so dangerous. EVAs are also difficult because the bulk of the spacesuit, space gloves, and helmet is clumsy. Movement in the weightlessness of space is also awkward and difficult. It's a little like floating in water, but without the resistance that water provides.

Both McDivitt and White were nervous. McDivitt grabbed at the hatch to keep it from opening too far. He knew if the hatch jammed,

---

* An orbit is determined by Earth's gravity and the momentum of the spacecraft. When McDivitt used the thrusters, he added to the spacecraft's momentum. That increase in momentum automatically increased *Gemini 4*'s altitude and changed its orbit. Flying a capsule in space was a lot different from flying a jet in Earth's atmosphere. The astronauts would need some new tricks for dealing with these differences.

they would never make it back to Earth alive. Meanwhile, White prepared to exit the spacecraft. He checked his camera, worried that he might forget to remove the lens cap. "I knew I might as well not come back if I did," he joked later. Finally, after 12 minutes of preparation with the hatch open, the first American EVA began. Ed White floated out of the hatch into the airlessness of space, while Jim McDivitt watched from inside the spacecraft and took some of the most memorable photos in history.

Ed White performs the first U.S. EVA during the *Gemini 4* spaceflight.

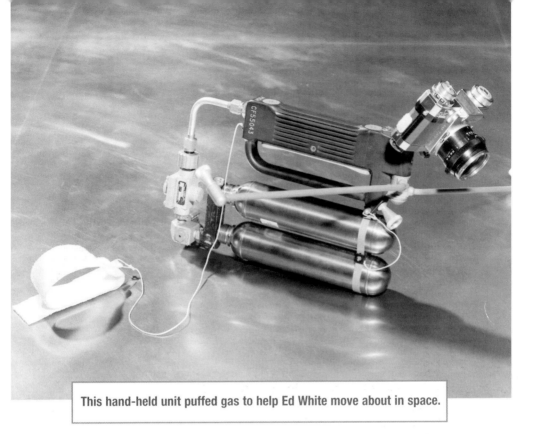

This hand-held unit puffed gas to help Ed White move about in space.

NASA engineers had studied film of Leonov's space walk and had noticed he seemed to have difficulty getting around. So they developed a little rocket gun for White, a handheld unit that blew puffs of gas wherever it was pointed. White could use this little rocket to move about outside.

A long connecting hose extended from White to the Gemini spacecraft, like a gold-colored umbilical cord—passing oxygen, communications, and power to the astronaut. (The brilliant gold color came from its Mylar coating, used to insulate the hose against the Sun's infrared radiation.) White also had a tether he could use to change his position. "Changing my position by pulling on the tether was easy," he later remarked, "like pulling a trout, say a 2- or 3-pounder, out of a stream on a light line."

As Earth floated below him, he reported to McDivitt and the ground crews, "I can sit out here and see the whole California coast." He was traveling alongside Gemini at a speed of about 17,500 miles (28,000 km) per hour. White had some difficulty avoiding the spacecraft, though. Once he started in one direction, it was hard to put on the brakes. The spacecraft was also harder for McDivitt to control as White moved about outside pulling on the umbilical cord and tether.

Spectacular views floated by, especially over Florida. "Looking down," White said later, "I could see all the lower part of the state, the island chain of Cuba, and Puerto Rico." McDivitt's stunning photos of

A view of the Florida Strait taken from *Gemini 4*

Ed White in space evoke the beauty and excitement of the moment. Finally, Flight Director Chris Kraft in Houston ordered McDivitt to tell White to come in. "This is fun," White responded, but he came back in.

Coming in was easier said than done, however. White had to struggle with his inflated suit and—despite his excellent physical condition—he was exhausted by the time he made it back to his seat inside and closed the hatch behind him. The EVA was over, and it was a success. Ed White had spent 21 minutes walking in space, twice as much time as Leonov. When White and McDivitt returned to Earth, there were parades and bands and celebrations. It was Project Gemini's greatest triumph.

Unfortunately, these were not generally good days for the space program. In 1963, President John F. Kennedy was assassinated in Dallas, Texas, and Vice President Lyndon Johnson took his place. Always before a NASA supporter, Johnson now became less friendly. The United States had become embroiled in an unpopular and costly war in Vietnam, and it was going poorly. Student riots and anti-war demonstrations raged all over the United States. Plagued by political and financial pressures, Johnson cut back NASA's budget. During the early days of the Gemini program, public support had also waned. But following White's successful EVA, Project Gemini suddenly caught the American imagination.

Johnson came to Houston to greet the astronauts personally, and a million people attended a ticker-tape parade in Chicago, Illinois. At Johnson's request, the astronauts also attended the Paris International Air Show, where they met Yuri Gagarin, the first human in space and the Soviet Union's first cosmonaut.

Health Hazards

Space is not a natural habitat for human beings—far from it—and as U.S. astronauts extended their missions in space, some of the negative effects began to become real concerns. Loss of bone mass soon became recognized as a major problem. Additionally, in weightlessness, blood pools in the legs and muscles grow weak from inactivity.

Movement is easy in space without the tug of gravity on the body. So the more time astronauts spend in space, the weaker their muscles become. That includes the most essential muscle, the heart. McDivitt and White were in space long enough for this to begin to present a problem, so doctors had suggested an exercise program. The question was: How could they exercise in such a cramped space? The *Gemini 4* astronauts used bungee cords and elastic for some limited exercise.

Pauline Beery Mack: Bone Seer

In the 1890s, when Pauline Beery Mack was growing up in Missouri, few women went to college. Even fewer became scientists. However, Mack earned a Ph.D. and became a respected researcher in chemistry, setting up high-tech research programs to study bone density, or bone mass, at what is now known as Texas Woman's University.

NASA became interested in Mack's work because astronauts lose bone mass in space. Gemini astronauts were the first U.S. astronauts to spend several days in space, and NASA doctors were worried about bone loss. In the 1960s, Mack started working with NASA on this problem.

She set up bed-rest studies to mimic what happens when a human experiences zero gravity. Volunteers remained motionless in bed—no sitting, standing, or moving about. It was the closest she could come on Earth to the effects of zero gravity. Mack designed X-ray equipment for "seeing" the loss of calcium and phosphorus in their bones. Based on her findings, she developed special diets to offset the loss of these minerals from the astronauts' bones.

In 1970, NASA astronauts awarded Pauline Mack the Silver Snoopy Award for her professional excellence and outstanding contributions to the space program. She was the first woman ever to receive the award.

The Gemini 4 mission lasted only a few days, but some astronauts now stay in space for weeks at a time. The need for useful forms of exercise has posed a continuing concern for long-duration space missions.

"Eight Days in a Garbage Can"

Aboard *Gemini 4*, McDivitt and White had spent an impressive 4 days in space, but $2\frac{1}{2}$ months later (August 21–25, 1965), Gordon Cooper and Charles "Pete" Conrad doubled that time. *Gemini 5* became their home and workplace for 8 days.

They experienced a longing for baths or showers, the scratchiness of stubbly beards, restlessness, and boredom. They also had a problem that no one had thought to deal with—garbage. Two people can generate a lot of waste in 8 days. What were they supposed to do with it? They also had another garbage-related problem—anything they left loose ended up floating aimlessly around the crew cabin.

Conrad said he passed the time wrapping and re-wrapping items to keep them secure so that crumbs, droplets, and other objects and bits of objects wouldn't end up floating all over the spacecraft. By the end of the mission, the garbage problem had become significant. That's why Conrad likes to refer to the Gemini 5 mission as "8 days in a garbage can."

The press, however, handled the *Gemini 5* mission with great enthusiasm. At last the United States might have a chance to pull in front in the space race. The longest Soviet flight so far had been in 1963, when cosmonaut Valery Bykovsky orbited Earth 81 times between June 14 and June 19. Now the United States would surpass that record.

Twenty-five reporters from the Associated Press covered the *Gemini 5* liftoff, and a vacant lot near the homes of Cooper and Conrad became a campsite for reporters who were eager for a scoop. Some may even have waited like vultures for failure, thinking that Cooper and Conrad might die from the long, 8-day exposure to space and its weightlessness. The Gemini 5 mission patch bore a covered wagon, and its unofficial mission motto—suggested by Cooper and vetoed by NASA—was "8 Days or Bust."

Shortly after liftoff, the mission met with some trouble. The fuel cells aboard the craft provided the primary electrical supply by converting hydrogen and oxygen into water and electricity. Because the mission was so long, Cooper was planning to operate the cells at very low pressure, but the pressure had suddenly dropped much too low. The astronauts tried to raise the pressure by heating the oxygen, but the pressure kept dropping. Keeping a watch on the problem, Cooper went ahead with the next stage in the mission plan, releasing a pod they would use for rendezvous exercises. He then used radar to track it.

In the meantime, the fuel-cell problem was getting worse, and the spacecraft was too far out of communications range to get advice. Cooper decided to power down, fearing they would lose power completely. Powered down, they couldn't rendezvous with the pod, and Cooper had to abandon the entire exercise. For a while, Flight Director Chris Kraft considered bringing *Gemini 5* down early. It was beginning to look as if the mission might be a "bust," after all. At one point, Conrad drew a sketch on the console of a covered wagon headed over a cliff. *Gemini 5* might not last more than 1 day in space.

As it turned out, though, the electrical power supply was not as big a problem as everyone feared. During the flight, the manufacturer had quickly set up some emergency tests to see how dangerous the situation really was. The tests showed that the fuel cells would still work on low pressure. Mission Control had Cooper and Conrad turn electrical power back on slowly, one item at a time. It all worked. The Covered Wagon would stay aloft for at least a little longer, and Cooper and Conrad tried to get some sleep.

With the rendezvous pod gone, Mission Control and the astronauts came up with a way to accomplish some of their goals, anyway. On the third day they set up a "phantom" rendezvous target. Kraft told Cooper an exact position, and Cooper guided Gemini to rendezvous with the position. He was able to do some fine flying, controlling the

Scientists and engineers in the Mission Operations Control Room monitored every detail of the Gemini flights. These workers are overseeing the Gemini 5 mission.

spacecraft expertly and using the entire control system. It was more precision than anyone had ever accomplished in space. The phantom method worked, and established new confidence in the astronauts' ability to rendezvous.

On the fifth day of their mission, Cooper and Conrad began to lose orbital control, and the astronauts had to drift for the rest of the mission. Worst of all, there was nothing to do. Now boredom really set in. They had set out to check on the effects—both physical and mental—of prolonged space flight, and they found out it was boring. Most Gemini missions were shorter—3 or 4 days—and the astronauts' days were filled with experiments and challenges. The Gemini 5 mission was entirely different.

As Pete Conrad described it later, "The fact is you can't do anything. You can't go anywhere. You can't move and have no great desire to sleep because you're not doing anything to make you tired. You don't have anything to read and there isn't any music." Even the great view gave out on them. As the mission neared its end, they were no longer able to use their thrusters to point the spacecraft, and so the spacecraft pointed itself. As luck would have it, the direction it pointed in never seemed to display anything of interest in the Gusmobile's two windows. The psychological challenges were probably the most difficult ones for the astronauts onboard *Gemini 5*.

By the end of the mission, Cooper and Conrad had set a new world record, 190 hours, 55 minutes, and 14 seconds in space. When it came time to leave space, however, a hurricane was hovering over their original landing site, so they changed their landing target. Their splashdown was 80 miles (129 km) short of their new target, but it could have been a lot worse if Cooper hadn't used

Gordon Cooper and Pete Conrad receive a red-carpet welcome home aboard the *USS Lake Champlain*.

manual-descent controls to offset a computer error he noticed in their path of descent.

Like McDivitt and White, Cooper and Conrad had lost calcium from their bones, blood plasma, and weight. However, within 2 days they had recovered completely, and the NASA physicians were greatly relieved.

The two astronauts had flown a marathon mission, and in the process, they had proved that precise rendezvous—even a ghost rendezvous!—was possible and that humans could endure as many as 8 days in space without real danger to their health. These were key accomplishments on the Gemini list of "musts."

Chapter 5

Nose-to-Nose in Space

The next three Gemini missions closed in on three of the most important questions that Project Gemini had set out to solve: Could astronauts stay in space long enough to go to the Moon, land, explore, and safely return? Could astronauts control two spacecraft precisely enough to rendezvous safely in very close proximity? Could one spacecraft dock safely with another during spaceflight?

With *Gemini 4*, NASA had doubled the previous length of stay in space to 4 days and doubled it again with *Gemini 5*. So far, so good. However, NASA engineers calculated that a trip to the Moon and back could take as long as 14 days, allowing for delays. What if that happened—and it was too much? If the astronauts got into trouble, they would be too far away to be brought back quickly. NASA wanted to make sure that the maximum time would not harm the astronauts. In Earth orbit, *biosensors* hooked up to the astronauts would warn physicians and scientists of trouble, and ailing astronauts could be rescued. So the astronauts of *Gemini 7* would now go into space for 14 days.

   Gemini 6 would demonstrate rendezvous with a spacecraft, and finally, *Gemini 8* would set out to show what could be done when two spacecraft were docked.

Tandem Mission

Aboard *Gemini 6*, astronauts Wally Schirra and Tom Stafford hoped to finally show that an astronaut could neatly guide a spacecraft to rendezvous and dock with another vehicle. This had to be proved, and so far, previous attempts had failed.

Tom Stafford (left) and Wally Schirra (right)—suited up and ready for their Gemini 6 mission

NASA decided to set up the first double launch. The target vehicle would go first—with no passengers. The target vehicle was called Agena, but really it was just an upper stage rocket with a restartable engine and a *docking adapter*. It was launched atop an Atlas rocket. Schirra and Stafford would follow aboard *Gemini 6* right afterward, if the Agena launch was successful.

Agena mounted atop its Atlas launch vehicle, prior to liftoff October 25, 1965

Wally Schirra: The "Astronaut's Astronaut"

Wally Schirra became known by many as the "astronaut's astronaut." He is the only one who flew in all three programs—Mercury, Gemini, and Apollo. Remembered as the astronaut who flew Mercury's "textbook mission" aboard *Sigma 7*, he had a fine hand at the controls.

Like many of the astronauts, Schirra was a military test pilot before he joined NASA. He was a graduate of the U.S. Naval Academy and, on loan to the U.S. Air Force, he flew ninety combat missions over Korea. His courage earned him the Distinguished Flying Cross.

Schirra's intelligence and sense of humor have made him a favorite guest commentator for many television news networks covering space activities. He has written about his experiences in his book, *Schirra's Space*.

Josephine Schirra pins NASA's Distinguished Service Medal on her husband, Wally Schirra, during a ceremony at the Pentagon in Washington, D.C.

It wasn't. The two astronauts were all set, suited up and in place inside the *Gemini 6* capsule. It was October 25, 1965. The Atlas rocket roared, and, together with Agena it lifted off smoothly. The two separated, and the Agena fired to move into orbit. But the target vehicle wobbled and then disintegrated. Schirra and Stafford wouldn't be going anywhere farther than home to Houston on that day.

Schirra was livid. Someone asked Stafford later what his partner had said when he heard the Agena had fizzled on them. Stafford smiled and said, "Something like 'Gosh darn, it's been a bad day.'"

The special features of the Agena target vehicle took time to install, and another Agena would not be ready for months. Schirra and Stafford returned to Houston, greatly let down, when they were called into a meeting. Gemini program manager Chuck Mathews had an idea. Why not launch *Gemini 6* during the next planned mission—Gemini 7 in December—and use the other Gemini spacecraft as a rendezvous target? Schirra and Stafford liked the idea a lot.

That's how *Gemini 6* became *Gemini 6-A* (same crew, same spacecraft—slightly different mission). It was launched in December, a few days after the long-duration *Gemini 7* flight. *Gemini 6-A* would zoom into space, rendezvous with *Gemini 7*, and then come home—leaving the *Gemini 7* crew to finish up their 14-day mission.

In for the Long Haul

When Frank Borman and Jim Lovell sat atop the big Titan II rocket on December 4, 1965, they knew they faced a record 14 days in the small, cramped cabin.

Of all the Gemini spacecraft, *Gemini 7* was the heaviest, requiring 430,000 pounds (195,045 kg) of thrust to raise it into Earth orbit. (As Borman once pointed out, by comparison, the four engines on a Boe-

Gemini 7 astronauts James Lovell (front) and Frank Borman (back) leave the suiting trailer during the pre-launch countdown.

Frank Borman and Jim Lovell petitioned NASA for permission to take reading material along on their 2-week trip into space. NASA gave permission for one paperback each, although they found that stowing the two books in the cramped quarters wasn't easy.

Borman chose to take a book called *Roughing It* by Mark Twain, a tale about a trip in the 1800s, and Lovell selected *Drums Along the Mohawk* by Walter Edmonds, a novel about wars between settlers and Native Americans in the eighteenth century.

Reading time turned out to be scarce, but their choices must have contrasted greatly with their weightless experiences orbiting high above Earth's surface.

ing 747 have a combined thrust of less than half that.) For *Gemini 7*, NASA used a modified Titan that had more thrust, but according to Borman, no one was really sure it was enough until the moment of liftoff. The moment came, the modified Titan did the job, and the Gemini capsule headed for space.

Gemini 7 accomplished its mission. It stayed in space for 2 weeks. That record remained unbroken for 5 years. Astronaut Frank Borman, who commanded the Gemini 7 mission, joked that it was like spending 2 weeks in the front seat of a Volkswagen Beetle. "Almost everything in the cabin was tiny," wrote Borman in his book *Countdown*, "including its two windows. It was simultaneously a workroom, kitchen, bathroom, and bedroom. . ." During the trip, the astronauts were scheduled to perform twenty experiments in this tiny space, in addition to the rendezvous with *Gemini 6-A*.

Meeting in Space

Gemini 6-A launched on December 15 and met up with *Gemini 7* in space. Wally Schirra maneuvered his spacecraft within 6 feet (2 m) of *Gemini 6-A* and hovered there for $5\frac{1}{2}$ hours.

Now the Gemini astronauts were beginning to take on even bigger challenges. NASA's space program, as astronaut Gene Cernan once wrote, was designed to move forward in baby steps, adding small new skills and capabilities one by one, piece by piece. Now, however, the Gemini astronauts were ready for one of their biggest challenges—rendezvous and *stationkeeping* between two piloted spacecraft. (Stationkeeping involves keeping two spacecraft at a constant distance from each other as they continue to orbit.) This was a big step, not just a traditional baby step, toward the coming flights to the Moon.

This photo of *Gemini 7* was taken from *Gemini 6-A* during rendezvous.

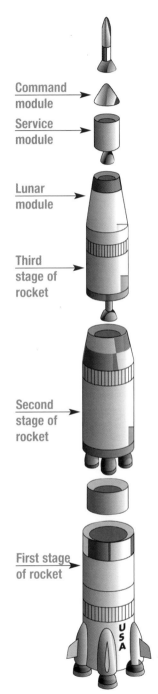

Command module

Service module

Lunar module

Third stage of rocket

Second stage of rocket

First stage of rocket

When astronauts headed for the Moon, they would travel in a specially designed three-part spacecraft. It would be made up of a *command module* (CM), a *service module* (SM), and a *lunar module* (LM). The lunar module was really a little lander spacecraft that could travel under its own power. In this little vehicle, two members of each three-person astronaut team would travel to the surface of the Moon. The third crew member would continue piloting the combined CM and SM (CSM) in orbit above the Moon's surface. Knowledge gained from the Gemini rendezvous and docking exercises was instrumental in deciding how the LM would be pulled away from—and return to—the Apollo CSM.

Schirra later remarked, "It was like the Blue Angels [formation jet fliers] at 18,000 miles per hour, only it was easier. There is no turbulence in space so there were no bumps in the road. Also the Gemini was magnificent to fly!" Even Schirra, famous for his piloting skills, was amazed at how well Gemini maneuvered. He flew around *Gemini 7*, "lit-

Apollo's three-part spacecraft rode into space atop the three stages of the big Saturn V rocket.

erally flying rings around it," he said, "and I could move to within inches of it in perfect confidence." The whole procedure required firing thrusters more than 35,000 times.

Up until then, no one had ever done this kind of flying in zero gravity, and no one had any experience to draw on. Wally Schirra was not only an expert jet flier, he was a very quick learner. Some of the skills these astronauts had gained as jet test pilots helped them, but they also had to learn new skills and be on their toes every moment. As Jim McDivitt had learned when he tried to speed up *Gemini 4* to catch an orbiting target, some maneuvers that made perfect sense in Earth gravity, just didn't work the same way in space.

Russian cosmonauts had brought their spacecraft within 3 miles (4.8 km) of each other and the newspapers had called it a "rendezvous." Schirra took exception to that description though. "No way was that rendezvous!" he said. "It was a passing glance . . ." It was the equivalent to catching sight of someone across the street, but by the time you try to say something, the person's gone. A real rendezvous, he implied, is more like having a date.

With the flights of *Gemini 6-A* and *7*, Project Gemini had flown two crewed missions at once—a first for the United States. The double flight wasn't part of the original plan, but it provided the rendezvous exercise NASA needed to prove once and for all that two spacecraft could meet in space. It also showed that NASA had the kind of flexibility that can turn a disappointing situation into a success.

This flexibility would prove priceless to NASA over and over—in both large dilemmas and small ones. A couple of years down the road, for example, flexibility and ingenious solutions saved the lives of three men in a life-threatening situation aboard the *Apollo 13* flight to the Moon.

Three Deaths

It had been 9 months since Leonov's *Voskhod 2* space-walking mission in March 1965, and nothing had been heard from the Soviet Union. One reason, as later became apparent, was that the Soviets were focused on building the new Soyuz spacecraft and setting up space stations. However, both plans and work had also progressed on the Soviet Moon program.

What did not become immediately apparent, however, was that the Soviets' chief engineering designer was seriously ill. Everyone was taken by surprise when Sergei Korolev died on an operating table on January 14, 1966. In some ways the Soviet program would never

Sergei Korolev, chief engineering designer for the Soviet space program, died unexpectedly in 1966.

completely recover from the loss of Korolev, whose existence was completely shrouded in mystery until his death. Then, suddenly, Soviet leaders revealed his name and gave him a state funeral. NASA sent astronaut Frank Borman to attend the chief designer's funeral. On the way there, Borman learned he would not be admitted, so he went back home. The Soviet Union's space program was anything but open or public.

A few weeks later, NASA lost the crew members who were originally scheduled to fly the Gemini 9 mission. On February 28, Elliot See and Charles Bassett were flying into Lambert Field in St. Louis, Missouri. They planned to visit McDonnell Aircraft Corporation, where their spacecraft was being built. Bad weather caused poor flying conditions, and See, who was flying the plane, misjudged the airstrip. When he circled back for a second approach, the plane struck the roof of the McDonnell building where workers were assembling the *Gemini 9* spacecraft. Several people were injured, and both See and Bassett were killed.

The Giant Video Game

Meanwhile, Neil Armstrong and David Scott were preparing for their Gemini 8 mission. Wally Schirra, the pilot of *Gemini-6A*, had proved that rendezvous could be done "Blue Angel"-style in space, but he didn't get a chance to dock. That challenge was the primary goal for *Gemini 8*. This time, the astronauts would try using Agena again. This time, it had to work.

The Agena experiments were exciting and challenging. "Docking in space is cool," Dick Gordon once remarked. He was a former Navy test pilot, and he thought docking with the Agena was a lot like air-to-

Docking to an Empty Spacecraft

The Agena system is sometimes called a rocket, sometimes called a satellite, and sometimes called a spacecraft. That's because it's really all those things at once—and no one seems to have a name for that.

An Agena is an upper-stage rocket that's often used in multistage rockets for launching satellites. It generally fires after the main rocket—usually an Atlas or Thor rocket. However, it can also function as a satellite itself. Additionally, it has a restartable rocket engine.

All these features made Agena a perfect choice when Project Gemini needed a docking "target." Gemini mission managers often called it a GATV—Gemini-Agena Target Vehicle.

At one end of the Agena, a rendezvous cone and "V" seat provided a docking site for the Gemini spacecraft. The crews could guide their craft up to the Agena and lock it into place, creating a two-part spacecraft.

Both command pilot and pilot could maneuver the Agena from controls on either side of the Gemini cockpit. The astronauts sent signals to the Agena using a coder that "talked" to the Agena computer. In this way, the astronauts could "drive" the Agena by remote control—changing its direction, starting up its big engine, and so on.

This photo of the Agena docking target was taken from *Gemini 8* during rendezvous.

air refueling in a plane. "You get yourself lined up," he said, "maybe 5 to 10 feet out. And if everything looks all right, and you look lined up with the docking cone, all you do is add a little thrust with the translational controller. And if it looks like you're going too fast you take a little off with the translational controller." It was an art, done by eyeballing the target and maneuvering "by feel." The Gemini astronauts were supreme artists when it came to guiding spacecraft.

Neil Armstrong was no exception. For the Gemini 8 mission, the two spacecraft were launched separately on the same day. This time the Agena launch went smoothly. Six hours after launch, *Gemini 8* pulled up to the Agena, then hovered 24 inches (61 cm) away. Armstrong eyed his target, then slowly eased Gemini into the Agena docking adapter. Tension was high in the little cabin as the two spacecraft touched. Then the latches snapped into place and the two spacecraft were joined. They had done it! *Gemini 8* and Agena were docked, and everything had gone perfectly.

Or had it? Suddenly the two spacecraft began to shift. Then they began to buck. Armstrong and Scott eyed Gemini's narrow docking nose. What if the docking assembly broke? The crew quickly detached their spacecraft from the Agena and backed carefully away, but Gemini's bucking didn't stop—in fact, it got much worse. The problem was obviously located in the Gemini spacecraft, not the Agena! The Agena had actually been stabilizing Gemini.

Finally, Armstrong and Scott realized that one of the rocket thrusters was firing out of control. They regained control by countering with their reentry thrusters. Once stabilized, they were able to shut down the system for maneuvering the spacecraft. Almost 75 percent of their fuel had been wasted.

Gemini 8 carried astronauts Neil Armstrong and David Scott into space.

Armstrong and Scott had to abandon the rest of their mission and make an emergency landing—it was the first Gemini landing in the Pacific Ocean. Their mission was cut short, but they had accomplished their most important goal, docking in space. It was a big step forward.

Chapter 6

Final Maneuvers

etween June and December 1966, Project Gemini would fly its last four missions. By early 1967, Project Apollo was expected to begin its flights and the Gemini Project had to be ready with all the answers to the questions posed for Apollo. Several questions remained.

First and most urgent, could long EVAs be done safely? Apollo astronauts would be walking on the Moon, exploring its surface, and clambering in and out of the lunar module. They also might need to take care of repairs outside the spacecraft on the voyage to or from the Moon. So far, Ed White had spent only 21 minutes walking in space, and found climbing back into the spacecraft an exhausting ordeal. Since then, so many other problems had cropped up that the Gemini astronauts had not had another chance at EVA yet, and a lot more needed to be known.

Second, were rendezvous and docking maneuvers well enough understood that the procedures could be done successfully every time? Also, could astronauts maneuver two docked spacecraft together? Could they be moved, for example, from one orbit to another? The Gemini astronauts needed to put Gemini and Agena through a few more paces.

The Scariest Spacewalk

Two months after Neil Armstrong and David Scott's successful docking mission, Tom Stafford and Gene Cernan took their places on May 17 in the *Gemini 9-A* spacecraft. It was the Gemini 9 mission that Elliot See and Charles Bassett would have flown.

The original *Gemini 9* crew, astronauts Elliott See and Charles Bassett

However, no Gemini launch took place that day. The Agena docking target failed to reach orbit. This was Tom Stafford's second experience with a fickle Agena—his first was with Wally Schirra during the Gemini 6 mission. This time Stafford was in the commander's seat.

The Gemini 9-A mission would have to wait another month. When liftoff finally took place in June, docking would still elude the unlucky mission. The Agena had made it to orbit this time and all looked good from the ground. But when Stafford and Cernan caught sight of their target, it seemed to be laughing at them. The shroud that was supposed to protect the docking apparatus during flight should have dropped away as the Agena reached orbit. Instead it had stuck partway on and partway off—looking like the gaping jaws of an alligator. Stafford and Cernan could rendezvous but they could not dock.

Gene Cernan broke all EVA records with a 2-hour space walk aboard *Gemini 9-A*. The plan was ambitious. Cernan clambered across the Gemini spacecraft, across the retrorocket section, and back to the adapter section. With his oxygen and communications lifeline trailing behind him, he used a small railing on the spacecraft skin to guide his progress.

When Cernan arrived at the back, he saw the jagged metal edge where the last rocket stage had dropped away. No one had thought about this hazard. A slice through his protective suit or his oxygen tube, and he would be dead. Cernan resourcefully worked out a way to protect his lifeline from the razor-sharp metal and leaped over it to the back of the adapter section. There he found the backpack propulsion system that was stowed away for him to use. However, he now ran into even more serious difficulties.

Eugene Cernan went on to fly two more space missions. As lunar module pilot of *Apollo 10*, he tested the LM by flying it to within 9 miles (14.5 km) of the Moon's surface. *Apollo 10* was a test mission, however, and Cernan was not actually permitted to land! He later had his chance to step onto the surface of the Moon aboard *Apollo 17*. As spacecraft commander of that mission, he spent more than 73 hours on the Moon's surface. It was the last of the Apollo Moon missions, and Cernan was last person to leave his footprints there.

Gene Cernan (seated) with fellow Apollo astronauts Harrison Schmitt (right) and Ron Evans (left) pose for this lunar rover shot prior to their Apollo 17 mission.

As he struggled to put on the backpack, his pulse rate climbed dangerously high. He also became overheated and his visor fogged up so badly that he couldn't see. Cernan had to cut the EVA shorter than originally planned. He knew he was lucky to make it back to the hatch alive.

Cernan was not at alone in his difficulties. As Soviet cosmonaut Alexei Leonov once remarked after his own EVA in March 1965, "I think that it is a bit too early to compare outer space with a place for an entertaining stroll . . . "

New Parking Zone

Six weeks later, John Young and Michael Collins set out on *Gemini 10.* They had better luck than Tom Stafford and Gene Cernan. It was only a 3-day flight, but this time, the Agena spacecraft cooperated, and in that short time, *Gemini 10* made a lot of progress.

First, Gemini docked with the Agena, which had been launched the same day as the *Gemini 10* liftoff. Part of the *Gemini 10* crew's job was to shift Agena by remote command to another orbit and park it there.

Gemini 10 astronauts John Young (left) and Michael Collins (right) pose with a model of the Gemini spacecraft.

Collins sent his digital instructions to the Agena engine, lit it up, and watched the fireworks. In a debriefing afterward, John Young explained, "At first, the sensation I got was that there was a pop, then there was a big explosion and a clang. We were thrown forward in the seats. Fire and sparks started coming out of the back end of that rascal. The light was something fierce and the acceleration was pretty good. . . I never saw anything like that before, sparks and fire and smoke and lights."

Once the Agena was fired up, Young used its engine, like a railroad switch engine, to move both spacecraft together to a different orbit— 474 miles (763 km) at its highest altitude. This was a record. Still attached to Agena, the astronauts bedded down in the new orbit. Later, they lowered the orbit and rounded it. Now they were orbiting near the Agena target used by *Gemini 8.*

That day, Collins made his first venture into space, a standup EVA, with just his torso outside the hatch. From this vantage, he photographed stars and the colors of space. Some unexplained fumes caused the astronauts' eyes to water, so they ended the session after about 50 minutes.

Later, Young separated from *Gemini 10*'s Agena target, tracked down the Agena target left behind by *Gemini 8*, and then rendezvoused with it. As soon as *Gemini 10* was close enough, Mike Collins set out on the major space walk of the mission—the first spacecraft-to-spacecraft EVA. At the end of a 50-foot (15-m) tether, Collins used a nitrogen gun to propel himself across to the Agena to collect a micrometeoroid experiment. Collins found that everything took longer than expected, an experience shared by Cernan.

When he got the experiment package, he found he had too few hands and little to hang onto. He used his nitrogen gun to position himself and clung to wire bundles and struts, while hanging onto the package. He finally got back to the spacecraft by pulling himself along the tether, hand over hand. Fuel was getting low, so the EVA ended there. Now, though, the lifeline snaked around inside the cockpit as though it were alive. Once detached from Collins, the astronauts opened the hatch one more time and tossed it out.

Gemini 10 splashed down in the Atlantic Ocean just 4 miles (6.4 km) from the recovery ship. One of the most successful Gemini missions had come to an end.

Earth Is Round

When Pete Conrad and Dick Gordon lifted off 2 months later, they immediately met up with their Agena target and docked with it. This was an excellent demonstration that rendezvous and docking could be done efficiently and on a schedule.

One of *Gemini 11*'s mission goals was to dock to the Agena, attach a 50-foot (15-m) nylon tether to both spacecraft, and carefully back away from the Agena until the tether line was taut. This, like all early EVA activities, was much easier said than done. At one point, Gordon was so exhausted in his struggle to attach the tether that he sat down astride the Agena cylinder to rest. Conrad, meanwhile, an exuberant cheerleader, was yelling, "Ride 'em, cowboy!" from inside the cockpit.

Once the tether was attached, Gemini began to spin in order to create artificial gravity in both spacecraft. This all went well up to the point where the tether was supposed to tighten between the two. Every

This view of the *Gemini 11* liftoff shows the erector frame that was lowered just prior to launch.

time Conrad tried to slowly back up his spacecraft, the Agena would follow. "If it hit you," he later observed dryly, "that could ruin your whole day." Conrad did finally get it right, by what he called real "seat-of-the-pants flying." The resulting spin created a very slight, but perceptible, amount of gravity inside Gemini. He described the effect as very comfortable.

The day before the mission ended, Conrad and Gordon got to see a sight no human being had ever seen before. They fired the Agena engine and it lit up with the display of what John Young had called "sparks and fire and smoke and lights." With that, Gemini and Agena shifted together, under Agena's rocket power, to a new orbit—and they set an altitude record of 853 miles (1,373 km). Conrad looked out the window and caught sight of Earth's spherical curve. "Houston, Eureka!" he exclaimed. "The world is really round."

Solving the EVA Problem

Gemini 12 got right down to business when it launched in November 1966. It docked and redocked with Agena. It did a manual docking with no assistance from ground control, and it effectively nailed down the remaining scenarios that Apollo astronauts needed to know about.

Beyond that, *Gemini 12*'s greatest contribution was to provide NASA with the first truly successful space walk. Space walks were not easy, and each experience proved that. By the time *Gemini 4*'s Ed White was safely back in the spacecraft, sweat was pouring down his face, his heart was pounding, and his faceplate was fogged. Eugene Cernan's efforts to put on his backpack had sent his pulse rate soaring during the Gemini 9-A mission. Aboard *Gemini 11*, Dick Gordon had become blinded by sweat while attaching a tether to the Agena spacecraft.

Pete Conrad: Third to Moon

Many of the astronauts found that few of their comments slipped by unnoticed. When Pete Conrad returned to Houston after *Gemini 11*, he found his mailbox stuffed with letters from members of the Flat Earth Society insisting that, despite what he may have seen from high above Earth, the planet is flat. They seemed to believe that what he had seen was just the round curve of a flat disk. Of course, much evidence has shown before and since that Earth is a ball-shaped sphere.

After his two Gemini missions (*Gemini 5* and *Gemini 11*), Conrad became commander of *Apollo 12* and the third astronaut to walk on the surface of the Moon. Later, after leaving NASA, he formed several companies involved in space commercialization. Conrad was killed in a motorcycle accident in 1999. He was 69.

Gemini 11 astronauts Pete Conrad (right) and Dick Gordon (left)

These problems were serious. What if Gordon had not been able to see and feel his way back to Gemini? What if Cernan had fainted? The astronauts knew that if one of them got into real trouble outside, the second would not be able to help. If he tried, both astronauts would be lost forever in space.

NASA engineers set out to find ways to cut down the dangerous levels of exertion required during EVAs. They also looked for ways to make weightlessness less frustrating—especially during a space walk. By now, NASA engineers were famous for solving critical problems with ingenious, practical solutions. The EVA problems were no exception.

When Jim Lovell and Buzz Aldrin flew the final Gemini mission, *Gemini 12*, they took along an array of specially designed gadgets to make EVA easier and much safer. During his EVA, Aldrin became the

During his *Gemini 12* EVA, astronaut Buzz Aldrin visited the Agena spacecraft.

first astronaut-mechanic. He installed an exterior handrail that he could hook up to by using nylon tethers attached to his spacesuit. He used rings on the exterior of the Agena to provide a stable position and free up his hands. He also attached portable Velcro handholds to the exterior of the spacecraft.

At a workshop area on Agena, he clamped into a restraint for his feet, again freeing his hands. There, he demonstrated that he could screw and unscrew bolts and manipulate connectors. He had no problems with overheating or raised pulse rates, and it looked like many of the scary EVA problems had been solved. At last, working in space began to look like a reality.

Heading Home: The Movie

As Aldrin and Lovell began their descent, they set in motion the exhilarating—and frightening—process of coming home. They were the tenth and last Gemini team to experience it. They activated the reentry thrusters around Gemini's slender nose and turned their spacecraft around, leading with the broad, flat base.

Next, they jettisoned part of the adapter section to free up the retrorockets that would begin slowing the spacecraft and kick it out of orbit. These four big engines ran on *solid fuel* and each packed a big 2,500-pound (1135-kg) punch. Timed by a state-of-the-art digital computer in Houston, the first one sprang to life, followed one-by-one by the other three. Together the retrorockets kicked in about one and a half times Earth's normal gravity, a real jolt for astronauts who had been flying in zero gravity for nearly 94 hours.

The *Gemini 12* crew, command pilot Jim Lovell (right) and pilot Buzz Aldrin, pose inside a model of the Gemini spacecraft. They are holding the camera equipment they used during the mission.

The retrorockets nudged *Gemini 12* out of orbit and into a shallow dive toward Earth's atmosphere. As the spacecraft's wide, blunt end began to lead the descent, the last segment of the adapter section was discarded. Now the protective heat shield was exposed, ready to do its highly important job. It would keep the astronauts and their spacecraft from frying in the intense heat that would begin to build up as they entered Earth's atmosphere.

Aldrin and Lovell worked over their checklist, making sure everything was done, as they said farewell to their high ride in the sky. Ten minutes later, the spacecraft began encountering the outer reaches of the upper atmosphere. The astronauts saw sparks of light as the spacecraft interacted with ions, or charged atoms, in the atmosphere. Strange, hazy orange shifted to dark green, and bright orange sparks flew through the thin air in a beautiful, spectacular display.

Meanwhile, the Gemini onboard computer began to do its job. While Jim Lovell was occupied with flying the spacecraft, Buzz Aldrin decided to record the descent on film. He had a 16-mm camera and found that he could hold it against the window to catch the view. Of course, during this time, the force of gravity was constantly increasing—and Aldrin had a hard time holding the camera steady. Finally he had to let go, but Aldrin had succeeded in capturing a rare sight.

Gemini 12 continued plummeting toward Earth. At 40,000 feet (12,192 m) the astronauts released the small drogue parachute designed to slow and steady the spacecraft. At 10,000 feet (3,048 m), the main parachute opened its 58-foot (17.7-m) umbrella.

As the astronauts prepared for splashdown, the *Gemini* spacecraft tilted up so that the wide end would hit the ocean first. This put Lovell and Aldrin in an upright position inside. Through the windows, they could see the water rush by, changing color as the capsule plunged downward and then bounced back up to the surface like a cork. The last Gusmobile had landed.

Chapter 7

From Gemini
to Apollo

Project Gemini had achieved all its goals within 5 years, and it passed on a wealth of experience and information to the Apollo astronauts and mission planners. The little two-seater spacecraft had done its job.

During its development and missions, Project Gemini employed more than 2 million people within NASA, in government agencies, and in private industry. The overall cost of the entire project was about $1.3 billion.

Not Trouble-Free

The Gemini missions all ended safely, and Americans breathed a sigh of relief and pride with each successful splashdown. The United States

The Gemini capsule proved sturdy and responsive during ten challenging piloted missions between March 1965 and November 1966.

really was showing the "right stuff"—sound engineering, careful planning, and a great deal of courage and skill. Looking back, however, historians recognize that some of that success also hinged on luck. No one knew then how to build a risk-free rocket and spacecraft—and we still don't know how today.

One Gemini crew ran low on fuel, and more than one missed a planned rendezvous. One spacecraft had a computer failure that required manual reentry. Other mechanical failures included a fuel cell that didn't work and two attitude thrusters that fizzled. Armstrong and Scott were placed in great danger when their spacecraft spun out of control as they tried to dock with Agena.

Despite these difficulties, no U.S. astronaut had yet died during a space mission. The Soviets had not been so lucky. Tragedy could also occur in the American space program, and every astronaut knew it. No one could afford to forget that space was dangerous. Traveling there would always be risky, and every trip held the possibility of death for those who dared to go. Yet, further travel and exploration in space seemed inevitable—a human endeavor for which the time had come.

The Moon: Now Within Reach

The Gemini missions made a place for the United States in space. Even more important in the long run, they extended the sum of human experience in space and set many milestones. During the Gemini flights, the astronauts were able to record an analysis of sleep in flight, perform cardiovascular exercises, measure how weightlessness and exposure to radiation affect the blood, and communicate with the ground during reentry.

The crews collected micrometeorites, learned to navigate in space by the stars, and measured surface features on Earth. They spent a total of 11 hours and 20 minutes floating outside their spacecraft. All these feats were important steps toward NASA's next big adventure: Humankind was headed for the Moon!

Gemini Mission Facts

Vital Statistics

Mission	Date of Launch	Astronauts	Highlights
GEMINI 1	April 8, 1964	None	Crewless test flight that orbited Earth for 4 days
GEMINI 2	January 19, 1965	None	18-minute suborbital test of the heat shield
GEMINI 3 (Molly Brown)	March 23, 1965	Gus Grissom, John Young	First truly piloted spacecraft flight
GEMINI 4	June 3, 1965	James McDivitt, Ed White	62 orbits, 4-day flight; Ed White makes first U.S. EVA
GEMINI 5	August 21, 1965	Gordon Cooper, Pete Conrad	New international record: 120 orbits, 8 days
GEMINI 7	December 4, 1965	Frank Borman, Jim Lovell	International duration record: 14 days, rendezvous with *Gemini 6-A*
GEMINI 6-A	December 15, 1965	Wally Schirra, Tom Stafford	Rendezvous with *Gemini 7*

Mission	Date of Launch	Astronauts	Highlights
Gemini 8	March 16, 1966	Neil Armstrong, Dave Scott	First docking of two spacecraft; linked spacecraft spin out of control, but safe emergency landing made
Gemini 9-A	June 3, 1966	Tom Stafford, Eugene Cernan	Cernan makes a 2-hour EVA
Gemini 10	July 18, 1966	John Young, Mike Collins	EVAs by Mike Collins; two rendezvous and docking maneuvers with Agena
Gemini 11	September 12, 1966	Pete Conrad, Dick Gordon	Two EVAs; reach a high orbit of 853 miles (1,373 km) while docked with the Agena target; artificial gravity experiment
Gemini 12	November 11, 1966	Jim Lovell, Buzz Aldrin	Three EVAs (the first truly successful ones); docking with an Agena target; artificial-gravity experiments; fully automated reentry

Project Gemini: A Timeline

1957 — The Soviet Union launches the first artificial satellite, *Sputnik 1.*

1958 — The United States launches its first satellite, *Explorer 1.*

1961 — The first piloted Mercury flight carries Alan Shepard into space aboard *Freedom 7.*

The McDonnell-Douglas Corporation in St. Louis, Missouri, receives the contract for the Gemini spacecraft.

1962 — John Glenn becomes the first U.S. astronaut to orbit Earth aboard *Friendship 7.*

1963 — In last Mercury flight, Gordon Cooper, aboard *Faith 7,* nearly quadruples the longest Mercury flight to date with 34.3 hours in space.

1965 — *Gemini 3,* the first piloted Gemini flight, is launched.

Aboard *Gemini 4*, Ed White performs first space walk by a U.S. astronaut.

Astronauts aboard *Gemini 5* set an 8-day international endurance record.

Gemini 6-A and *7* complete first close rendezvous in space.

1966 — *Gemini 8* and unpiloted Agena spacecraft perform the first successful docking exercise in space.

Eugene Cernan makes a 2-hour space walk aboard *Gemini 9-A*.

Gemini 10 and *Gemini 11* are launched.

Astronauts aboard *Gemini 12* perform the first truly successful EVAs.

Glossary

attitude—the position of a spacecraft in flight in relation to a fixed reference such as the horizon or another vehicle; also, a spacecraft's orientation with respect to the direction in which it is moving

biosensor—one of a group of electrodes used to track heartbeat, breathing, and other important body functions

command module (CM)—the main Apollo spacecraft module; it is the only part of the spacecraft that returned to Earth at the end of a mission

dock—to join with another spacecraft, like a ship coming into a dock to tie up; once docked, astronauts may be able to move from one spacecraft to another

docking adapter—a device that makes docking between two spacecraft possible

electrode—a solid conductor through which an electric current enters or leaves a fuel cell or battery

electrolyte—a substance that conducts electricity when dissolved or melted

extravehicular activity (EVA)—a space walk or other activity outside a spacecraft

intercontinental ballistic missile (ICBM)—a rocket developed for military purposes, but sometimes used for launching spacecraft

lift (noun)—upward motion; the force available for raising; the upward distance achieved

lunar module (LM)—the portion of the three-part Apollo spacecraft that was used to land on the Moon (the other two are the command and service modules)

multistage rocket—a rocket system that uses one or more booster rockets to provide additional lift

orbit—the path followed by an object in space as it revolves around another object in space

pitch—movement that causes the nose of a spacecraft to lift or descend in relation to the rear

rendezvous—(verb) to meet, to be in the same area at the same time; (noun) a meeting or encounter

satellite—an object that orbits another object. Natural satellites include planets, asteroids, or comets that orbit the Sun or a moon that orbits a planet or an asteroid. Many artificial satellites, such as the Sputnik and Gemini spacecraft, have been launched into space by humans.

service module (SM)—the portion of the Apollo spacecraft that carried fuel, supplies, and engines

stationkeeping—to keep two spacecraft at a consistent distance from each other as they continue to orbit

solid fuel—a fuel that is a powder or solid material, for example, gunpowder

thruster—a rocket positioned so that small bursts can control the movement of a spacecraft. A burst from the left thruster will nudge a spacecraft to the right. A short blast from the right thruster will send the spacecraft left. Rear thrusters can nudge or zoom a spacecraft forward.

To Find Out More

The news from space changes fast, so it's always a good idea to check the copyright date on books, CD-ROMs, and videotapes to make sure that you are getting up-to-date information. One good place to look for current information from NASA is U.S. government depository libraries. There are several in each state.

Books

Burrows, William. *This New Ocean: A History of the First Space Age.* New York: Random House, 1998.

Campbell, Ann Jeanette. *The New York Public Library Amazing Space: A Book of Answers for Kids.* New York: John Wiley & Sons, 1997.

Cernan, Eugene, with Don Davis. *The Last Man on the Moon.* New York: St. Martin's Press, 1999.

Hacker, Barton C., and James M. Grimwood. *On the Shoulders of Titan: A History of Project Gemini.* Washington, D.C.: NASA SP-4210, 1979.

Schefter, James. *The Race: The Uncensored Story of How America Beat Russia to the Moon.* New York: Doubleday, 1999.

Schirra, Wally, with Richard N. Billings. *Schirra's Space.* Annapolis, Md.: Naval Institute Press, 1995.

Slayton, Donald K., with Michael Cassutt. *Deke! U.S. Manned Space: From Mercury to the Shuttle.* New York: St. Martin's Press, 1994.

Spangenburg, Ray, and Diane Moser. *Exploring the Space Frontier.* New York: Facts On File, Inc., 1989.

_____. *Space People from A to Z.* New York: Facts On File, Inc., 1990.

CD-ROMs

Space: A Visual History of Manned Space Flight, Second Edition
Sumeria, Inc.
http://www.sumeria.com
100 Eucalyptus Drive
San Francisco, CA 94132

NASA Museum: A Tour Through America's Continuing Exploration of Space
Saturn Five
http://www.saturnfiveltd.com
6380 S. Eastern Ave., Suite 12
Las Vegas, NV 89120

Video Tapes

History of Spaceflight: Reaching for the Stars. Finley-Holiday Film Corp., 1995.

Mercury and Gemini Spacecraft Missions. Finley-Holiday Film Corp., 1988.

Organizations and Online Sites

Many of the sites listed below are NASA sites, with links to many other interesting sources of information about moons and planetary systems. You can also sign up to receive NASA news on many subjects via e-mail.

Astronomical Society of the Pacific
390 Ashton Avenue
San Francisco, CA 94112
http://www.aspsky.org/

The Astronomy Café
http://www2.ari.net/home/odenwald/cafe.html
NASA scientist Sten Odenwald answers questions and offers news and articles relating to astronomy and space.

Kennedy Space Center
http://www.ksc.nasa.gov/ksc.html
This site features an overview of shuttle flights as well as information about the Mercury, Gemini, and Apollo programs.

NASA Ask a Space Scientist
http://image.gsfc.nasa.gov/poetry/ask/askmag.html#list
NASA scientists answer your questions about astronomy, space, and space missions. The site also has archives and fact sheets.

NASA History
http://history.nasa.gov
This in-depth site has information about all aspects of NASA history.

NASA Human Spaceflight
http://spaceflight.nasa.gov/index-m.html
This is the Internet hub for exploring everything related to human spaceflight, including current stories and realtime data as they break. You can explore the International Space Station, track Space Shuttle flights, trace space history, and see many interesting images.

NASA Newsroom
http://www.nasa.gov/newsinfo/newsroom.html
This site has NASA's latest press releases, status reports, and fact sheets. It includes a NASA News Archive for past reports and a

search button for the NASA Web. You can even sign up for e-mail versions of all NASA press releases.

National Space Society
600 Pennsylvania Avenue, S.E., Suite 201
Washington, DC 20003
http://www.nss.org

The Planetary Society
65 North Catalina Avenue
Pasadena, CA 91106-2301
http://www.planetary.org/

Places to Visit

Check the Internet (*www.skypub.com* is a good place to start), your local visitors' center, or phone directory for planetariums and science museums near you. Here are a few suggestions:

Exploratorium
3601 Lyon Street
San Francisco, CA 94123
http://www.exploratorium.edu/
Internationally acclaimed interactive science exhibits, including astronomy subjects.

Jet Propulsion Laboratory (JPL)
4800 Oak Grove Drive
Pasadena, CA 91109
http://www.jpl.nasa.gov/faq/#tour
Tours available once or twice a week by arrangement; see web site for instructions, or write to the JPL visitor contact. JPL is the primary mission center for all NASA planetary missions.

NASA Goddard Space Flight Center
Code 130, Public Affairs Office
Greenbelt, MD 20771
http://pao.gsfc.nasa.gov/vc/info/info.htm
Visitors can see a Moon rock, brought back to Earth by Apollo astronauts, as well as other related exhibits.

Space Center Houston
Space Center Houston Information
1601 NASA Road 1
Houston, TX 77058
http://www.spacecenter.org/
Offers a tour and exhibits related to humans in space, including the Apollo missions to the Moon.

Spaceport USA
Kennedy Space Center
Titusville, FL 32899
http://www.ksc.nasa.gov/ksc.html
Museum and special exhibits on the history of space exploration.

U.S. Space and Rocket Center
P.O. Box 070015
Huntsville, AL 35807-7015
http://ussrc.com
Exhibits of meteorites and rockets, Spacedome IMAX Theater, full-scale mock-up of the Russian Mir space station, and home of the U.S. Space Camp, where participants learn by doing about space exploration and space science.

Index

Bold numbers indicate illustrations.

Ray Spangenburg and **Kit Moser** are a husband-and-wife writing team specializing in science and technology. They have written 33 books and more than 100 articles, including a five-book series on the history of science and a four-book series on the history of space exploration. As journalists, they covered NASA and related science activities for many years. They have flown on NASA's Kuiper Airborne Observatory, covered stories at the Deep Space Network in the Mojave Desert, and experienced zero-gravity on experimental NASA flights out of NASA Ames Research Center. They live in Carmichael, California, with their two dogs, Mencken (a Sharpei mix) and F. Scott Fitz (a Boston Terrier).

Pluto

Uranus

Jupiter

Mars

Mercury

Su